EFFECTIVE LEADERSHIP IN SMALL GROUPS

by Nathan W. Turner

Judson Press ®
Valley Forge

EFFECTIVE LEADERSHIP IN SMALL GROUPS

Copyright © 1977
Judson Press, P.O. Box 851, Valley Forge, PA 19482-0851
Third Printing, 1983

Library of Congress Cataloging in Publication Data
Turner, Nathan W.
   Effective leadership in small groups.

   Bibliography: p. 61.
   1. Small groups.   2. Leadership.   I.   Title.
HM133.T87   301.18′5   77-8411

The name JUDSON PRESS is registered as a trademark in the U.S. Patent Office.

Printed in the U.S.A. ⊕

*This book is dedicated to Marge, who has
expanded my knowledge of small groups by
her perceptive questions over the years.*

Acknowledgments

The author would like to acknowledge a number of persons whose influence on him over the years is reflected in some of his insights and statements. Although the author assumes full responsibility for the content of the book, it is with a spirit of appreciation that he acknowledges the following persons who have been positive and challenging influences on his insights into small groups:

Over the years American Baptists like Dr. LeRoy J. Day, Dr. Martha M. Leypoldt, Dr. Robert Dow, and Dr. Harold Frazee have shared personal insights which challenged the author to inquire further into the nature of small groups.

More recently, Dr. Edmund Amidon, Dr. Irene Casper, Dr. Tom Hawkes, and Dr. Patricia Minuchin of the department faculty in Psychoeducational Processes at Temple University have been especially helpful in challenging the author to think, write, and do further research in small group dynamics.

Personal conversations and shared leadership of groups with Dr. Kenneth L. Cober and Dr. William R. Stayton have been especially important influences in the development of this author's ideas concerning group leadership.

For these persons, and countless others, this author wishes to express a word of personal gratitude.

Contents

Introduction

This small book is intended as an introductory text for leaders, facilitators, and teachers of small groups within religious, voluntary, and other social organizations. Leaders of such groups have wanted to be effective in their small group leadership over the years. Consequently, this book is specifically focused on their leadership needs. Its brief chapters will guide the reader through general background information about small groups to more specific "how to do it" types of information.

Leaders of small groups can enable a group to identify what has been happening in the group in a number of ways:

1. The group leader can learn to trust his or her own feelings, hunches, and intuition and to share such feelings with the group.

2. The group leader can assist the group in analyzing its own behavior and in discovering what is happening within the group. A way to do such discovering is to invite feedback from the group in order to test out feelings and ideas.

3. The group leader can lead the group in analyzing the verbal content of what goes on, the particular stage of group development, the decision-making process and its effective functioning, and the degree of personal interest and involvement each member has in what has been happening.

4. The leader can ask for a discussion about what has *not* been happening and how the group feels about omissions and/or lack of progress. It is often wise to secure suggestions from members about how to change so progress can be made.

There will be numerous uses for this book. It may be used as a basic text and guidebook for leaders, facilitators, teachers, and group leaders. Teachers and leaders of youth and adult classes or groups may find it a valuable guide to keep handy. Workshop, seminar, and laboratory school leaders will find it helpful. Chapter 5, "Local

Church Workshops," is designed to be used by a church or group to train teachers and board and committee leaders. Professional group leaders desiring a brief book on small group facilitation and leadership will find it an introductory resource. Finally, anyone interested in small group leadership and the dynamics of small groups will find this book helpful.

CHAPTER 1

MAIN QUESTION "WHAT IS
THE PURPOSE?"
CLEARLY DEFING IT

Leading Effectively
in Groups

In order to lead a small group effectively, one needs to know something about the **context** of the group, the **norms** and **processes,** what goes into being a **group facilitator,** and the difference between **task and maintenance roles** which members provide. It will be the purpose of this first chapter to discuss these four areas.

Contexts of Groups

The context in which a group exists can influence its functions, its expectations, and the type of leadership it requires. Group contexts include the church, the home, camp and conference centers, coffeehouses, community organizations, family clusters, and other voluntary groups. Obviously there are many more contexts in which groups function, and this list is only suggestive.

Within a given context, both group leaders and group members may make assumptions about the group. When such assumptions are made, then personal expectations are formed by each individual. Too often these are not shared or checked. And when these assumptions and expectations begin to operate within the group process, confusion, misunderstandings, and conflict may arise unnecessarily. For example, say the group context is a family cluster. If I expect a lot of structure and organization, I can be frustrated and disappointed if the leader provides only minimal organization.

The context of a group includes the physical environment. The color of the room, the furnishings, the total decor, plus the color of the clothing of the group members all have an impact on the group's context. Furthermore, the time of day, the day of the week, and the weather (for example, overly warm and humid or overly cold and windy) can influence the group and the members' responses to one another.

An additional context for a group is its psychological or

emotional composition. For example, if the group comes into the room anticipating trouble, the group will likely find the trouble it was fearing. If a group enters a room anticipating a positive and productive session, it will likely experience much of what was anticipated. Some psychologists often say that we experience what we prophesy will happen. This process is often termed a "self-fulfilling prophecy." And such self-fulfilling prophecies can and do become part of the overall group context which influences how a group functions.

Group Norms

Groups typically have their own norms[1] by which they are known. Some group members tend to remain silent, thereby permitting a few talkative ones to do all the talking. Other groups may have members who are very talkative with only a very few members who do not participate verbally. A norm for certain groups is formality including the use of titles, taking action only by votes according to *Robert's Rules of Order,* and recording everything in the minutes.

Every member has a *responsibility* to help the group develop norms and functions which assist the group to be productive. An effective group will develop and operate on some or all of the following norms or standards:

1. *Acceptance.* Persons are accepting of other members rather than rejecting.

2. *Freedom of expression.* Persons feel free to express their ideas and feelings honestly and openly during times of agreement and disagreement.

3. *Member participation.* All members are encouraged to participate so as to feel included and to foster maximum exchange of ideas, information, and options.

4. *Listening.* Persons actively listen to each one who speaks by indicating that the person is understood and by asking questions which elicit more information when desired.

5. *Dealing with feelings.* Even in task groups, times occur when personal feelings need to be dealt with and resolved before further progress can be made.

[1] A group norm (or standard) means that group members tend to exhibit relative uniformity (similarity) in opinions and behaviors. That is, people are strongly influenced by the groups to which they belong.

Factors That Affect a Group

Certain factors are important for effective group functioning:

1. *Limit the size.* The size of the group for effective discussion needs to be kept at ten to twelve persons. If larger numbers are involved, then subdivide into groups of ten or less for the best discussion. Subgroups need *not* report back verbally unless the data will be used immediately.

2. *Make a contract.* Persons need to agree to *why* they are meeting (purpose), for *how long,* who is to *lead* and *record* actions, *who* will *carry out* the *decisions* (delegate responsibility), and *who* will *evaluate* the *process.*

3. *Clarify roles.* It is valuable to a group if the members clarify the roles of the leader(s) and group members and/or anyone else present so that everyone is clear on what to expect from each other.

The processes involved in a group are complex and often function silently rather than verbally. Symptoms signaling that something is amiss in the group include apathy, anger, boredom, impersonal comments, conflict avoidance, gross confusion, constantly asking to clarify the goals because they are unclear, persons vying for leadership, sexist jokes and comments which put down either sex, and inappropriate humor (that is, jokes at a serious time). When such symptoms appear, they are a message to the group leader or teacher that something is going on within the group which needs attention.

These symptoms mean the teacher or leader should become active by asking the group if something needs attention and helping them to identify the problem. The remaining chapters in this book will provide guidelines for the leader on how to deal with such symptoms in a group.

Basic Skills for Effective Group Leadership

Basic skills for effective leadership in groups include:

1. An ability to *listen* to others;

2. An ability to *summarize* where the group is;

3. An ability to *ask questions* in specific ways to guide the group in a needed direction;

4. An ability to *cope with conflict* when it arises and/or a willingness to elicit a hidden conflict when the group is avoiding it;

5. An ability to *be patient* when the group needs to struggle with an issue (without being rescued by a leader);

6. An ability to *distinguish* between our personal needs as leaders and the needs of the group (Ask: Am I meeting my needs at the expense of the group?);

7. An ability to *share leadership* functions within the group without being threatened that we will lose control of the group;

8. An ability to *facilitate* one member relating her or his contribution to another's idea in order to keep the discussion "building" in one direction;

9. An ability to *deal with* ideas, task, and feelings and develop a sense of timing when the *maintenance* of the group's life should be given priority over content or task;

10. An ability to be *comfortable* with group silence(s);

11. An ability to keep the group *focused on issues* rather than on personality;

12. An ability to help the group to do *problem solving* and *evaluation;*

13. An ability to *delegate responsibility;*

14. An ability to facilitate the group facing its own need to *terminate* when its task is finished;

15. An ability to enable the group to *set goals and revise* its goals when necessary;

16. An ability to *enable the group* to understand its own group process(es) and to learn from them.

Above all, an effective group leader needs to **facilitate** the group members' understanding of the task and maintenance roles needed to help a group be an effective group.

Understanding Member Roles: Task and Maintenance

A group, like an individual, needs the knowledge, skills, and equipment its job calls for. It needs, also, to be in good working condition—willing to work, confident, and alert. If a group is to reach and maintain high productivity, its members have to provide for two kinds of needs—one is what it takes to do the job and the other is what it takes to strengthen and maintain the group. These are functions which help to make the group cohesive.

Task Roles (functions required in selecting and carrying out a group task)

Initiating Activity: Proposing solutions, suggesting new ideas, new definition of the problem, new attack on problem or new organization of material.

Seeking Information: Asking for clarification of suggestions, requesting additional information or facts.

Seeking Opinion: Looking for an expression of feeling about something from the members, seeking clarification of values, suggestions, or ideas.

Giving Information: Offering facts or generalizations, relating one's own experience to the group problem to illustrate a point.

Giving Opinion: Stating an opinion or belief concerning a suggestion or one of several suggestions, particularly concerning its value rather than its factual basis.

Elaborating: Clarifying, giving examples or developing meanings, trying to envision how a proposal might work out if adopted.

Coordinating: Showing relationships among various ideas or suggestions, trying to pull ideas and suggestions together, trying to draw together activities of various subgroups or members.

Summarizing: Pulling together related ideas or suggestions, restating suggestions after the group has discussed them.

Testing Feasibility: Making application of suggestions to real situations, examining practicality and workability of ideas, pre-evaluating decisions.

Group Building or Group Maintenance Roles (functions required in strengthening and maintaining a group's life and helping it to stay together when the going is rough)

Encouraging: Being friendly, warm, responsive to others, praising others and their ideas, agreeing with and accepting contributions of others.

Gatekeeping: Trying to make it possible for another member to make a contribution to the group by saying, "We haven't heard anything from Jim yet" or suggesting a limited talking time for everyone so that all will have a chance to be heard.

Standard Setting: Expressing standards for the group to use in choosing its content or procedures or in evaluating its decisions, reminding the group to avoid decisions which conflict with group standards.

Following: Going along with decisions of the group, somewhat passively accepting ideas of others, serving as audience during group discussion and decision making.

Expressing Group Feeling: Summarizing what group feeling is sensed to be, describing reactions of the group to ideas or solutions.

Both Group Task and Group Maintenance Roles

Evaluating: Submitting group decisions or accomplishments to comparison with group standards, measuring accomplishments against goals.

Diagnosing: Determining sources of difficulties, appropriate steps to take next, the main blocks to progress.

Testing for Consensus: Tentatively asking for group opinions in order to find out if the group is nearing consensus on a decision, sending up trial balloons to test group opinions.

Mediating: Harmonizing, conciliating differences in points of view, making compromise solutions.

Relieving Tension: Draining off negative feeling by jesting or pouring oil on troubled waters, putting a tense situation in wider context.

Understanding Acceptance of Expressed Feelings: Freeing for further insight and participation.

The above listing describes a range of behavior which members of a group and the leader need to provide if the group is to be productive and satisfying. Any group is strengthened and enabled to work more effectively if the members:

1. Become conscious of the functional roles the group needs at any one time;

2. Find out the degree to which they are helping to meet these needs through what they do;

3. Undertake effective self training to improve their member-role behavior.

The "Task and Maintenance Function" Workshop in Chapter 5 can be useful in teaching a group these member roles. The chart in the Workshop can help a group check on the way it is functioning.

Summary

In this chapter a brief description of various group contexts was presented. A listing of desirable group norms (or standards) was included, with a discussion of the complexity of group processes. Basic skills for effective group leadership were listed for the convenience of the reader. Task and maintenance group member roles were also described.

CHAPTER 2

Stages of Group Development, or One Way to View a Group

The effective leader or teacher of small groups needs to understand the context of the group, something about group norms, the task and maintenance functions which help a group do its work, and basic communication skills. Moreover, a brief knowledge of the stages of group development and theoretical group models is basic for any leader.

Stages of Group Development

Groups go through predictable stages of development. A number of group theorists have developed organized steps of how to view a group's development over a period of time. Small group leaders or teachers are sometimes confused when some things occur in a group, but these are usually normal aspects of that group's growth. If one can understand some of the normal developmental steps through which a group struggles, then what often seems unusual or confusing behavior can be viewed as a routine step.

For example, most groups experience some degree of struggle over who will be the leader and who will influence the group significantly. Even if the group has an official leader, or chairperson, it is quite possible for others in the group to lead the group via informal means of influence. One form of informal influence is to create a possible doubt through the use of questions or silences. Such informal influence may or may not serve to undermine the leadership role of the designated leader or teacher of the group. Of course, direct, open influence on a group is ideal and is to be encouraged by all group members. It is helpful to a group for persons to indicate an open desire to influence the group discussion or decision-making process.

One of the best-known theories about how groups develop is called the I.C.A. theory. The letters represent Inclusion, Control, and Affection. The theory was developed by William Schutz. Let us now consider this theory as one way to view a group as it develops.

One Way to View a Group: The I.C.A. Theory

Schutz stated in his I.C.A. theory that all persons have three interpersonal needs when functioning within a small group. The three interpersonal needs are *inclusion (I), control (C),* and *affection (A).*[1]

Because these three needs operate within persons, Schutz felt that small groups must have the same three needs of inclusion, control, and affection functioning within the group. Over the years he discovered through his research that groups actually do move through these three stages of development; namely, *inclusion, control,* and *affection.* An alternate set of descriptive words might be acceptance, influence, and expression of strong feelings. Schutz also discovered that as a group begins to wind down and conclude its work, the stages reverse themselves: *affection, control,* and *inclusion.* The overview of the stages a group moves through may now be viewed as the following steps: *inclusion (I), control (C),* and *affection (A)* followed by the reverse cycle of *affection (A), control (C),* and *inclusion (I).*

By knowing this sequence of developmental steps, a group leader or teacher may anticipate certain dynamics and group problems. Certainly the group leader will understand that a group must go through the various steps of growth if it is to develop fully as a group. It is possible, however, for a group never to develop beyond the first step of inclusion (I). Such groups are often described as "failures" or "disappointing" experiences by both members and leaders. The next page portrays the various steps in the I.C.A. theory in graphic fashion.

According to Schutz, the basic concerns of a group focus on inclusion, control, and affection. When people in a group begin to focus on any one of these three concerns, the following questions illustrate the concerns shared in a typical group:

Inclusion: Who else is here?
How can I be in relation to them?
What will it cost to join this group?
How much am I willing to pay to become a member?
Can I trust my real self to them?
Will they support me if the going gets rough?
How can I get acquainted with them?

[1] See chapter 4 of William C. Schutz, *Joy: Expanding Human Awareness* (New York: Grove Press, Inc., 1968).

The Inclusion-Control-Affection Theory

by William Schutz

(Diagram by N. W. Turner)

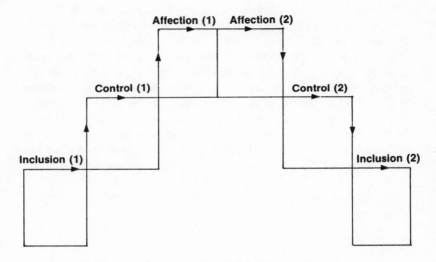

Control: Who is calling the shots here?
How much can I push for what I want?
Will I have to be direct or indirect to influence others?
What do others require of me?
Can I say what I really think and feel?
Can I take it if they say what they really think?

Affection: Am I willing to care?
Can I show my caring?
What will happen if I show I care for one person
before I show caring for others?
What if no one cares for me?
What if they do show caring for me?
What if I don't really ever care for someone in the group?
Will the group be able to bear it?
Is showing affection acceptable in this group? How do I
know this?

The I.C.A. way of viewing a group is a practical way to examine a church board, committee, or small group. Church groups are no different; meetings begin with members having the concerns listed under the inclusion section above. Certainly questions like "Who is here?"; "What is your name?"; and "Can I trust myself with this group?" are typical concerns in any church organization. Control concerns usually arise with questions like "Who is leading the meeting today?" and "How much will this group require of me?" Affectional concerns normally surface with questions like "Can I dare show caring for another member when we are focused only on the task before us?" and "Will the others in this group like me?"

When a group knows that its life must terminate, for instance, in a church board at the end of the church year when some members' term of office will be up, the I.C.A. process tends to reverse itself as A.C.I. During this closing out process, we usually see persons beginning to pull back from affectional ties which will have no future beyond the group; we see control concerns arise again expressed by "Who's boss here?" or "You don't have the right to make that decision now!" Finally, the inclusion concern arises again around questions of whether I (we) want to put time into the efforts of this class, group, board, or committee and its future work. After all, what's the use?

In viewing a group from the I.C.A. framework, it is important to realize that *all these concerns overlap* during the life of a group. This is especially so if a new member enters the group, a member leaves, or the group experiences a trauma. Certainly one of the three concerns may predominate; yet the other two concerns may be slightly in evidence in minor or subtle ways.

Summary

This chapter has presented basic background information on the fact that groups move through stages of development which are predictable. The importance of the individual's influence in a group was noted.

The major part of the chapter was devoted to the I.C.A. way of viewing a group as developed by William Schutz. Key questions in the three areas of group concern under *inclusion, control,* and *affection* were presented for the reader's convenience in relating the model to local church groups. A chart showing the three stages and how they reverse themselves was also included.

CHAPTER 3

Leadership in Groups

Leadership is an interesting and occasionally confusing word. What does it really mean? What are its implications in small groups? Is leadership always by a certain kind of person?

Leadership is traditionally considered to be exercised by a certain type of person leading a group in a particular manner. The usual types of leadership roles within groups or organizations include president, vice-president, secretary, and treasurer. Clearly, authority is traditionally vested in the specific leader role or position.

Leadership is a *function* of specific influence occurring within a group. Leadership is a particular *role* assigned, delegated, or given by others in the group to a person or persons within a group or organization. Leadership is a *process* involving two or more persons in a group for the purpose of attaining common goals. Leadership is a *set of interpersonal skills learned* (or acquired) by a person who is interested in developing his or her ability to influence others. Finally, leadership assumes an ability to *communicate clearly* with others and to be able to cope with the mutual dependency engendered between leader and follower(s).

In order to be clear on what this chapter is about, let it be stated herein that *leadership is primarily a function and responsibility of the total group.* Consequently, a group may function without a leader (often called "leaderless" groups) officially and perform very well indeed. Chapter 1 in this book details many of the basic leadership functions provided by members in a group if effective work is to be done. A major shift in the field of social psychology in recent years affirms the view that *leadership is a set of learned skills* rather than a set of characteristics bestowed on one person alone. For years churches and religious institutions have been oriented toward dramatic types of leaders who can preach, teach, lead, and/or entertain persons with their "charisma."

The dependence of religious groups and organizations on such personality types fostered an era of feeling that "our group cannot meet or decide anything until our leader arrives." A new era began some years ago with the use of leaderless groups, the employment of varied small group methods (like meeting in twos, threes, fours), and the acceptance of the idea that leadership is a group responsibility.

The theory of functional leadership contains two basic ideas: (1) any member of the group may assume the leadership of the group by performing actions that fulfill group functional needs, and (2) every leadership function may be fulfilled by a variety of group members serving various group needs with their specific behaviors (like asking questions or making supportive statements).

In 1939, Lewin, Lippitt, and White researched three leadership styles which were named autocratic, democratic, and laissez-faire. The *autocratic* leader decided all policy and gave all orders to group members. The *democratic* leader encouraged group determination of policy and enabled the group to interact within itself. The *laissez-faire* leader provided very minimal leadership for the group and interacted with group members in only a marginal or average manner. Most of the research upheld the democratic leadership style as the most effective. Yet, different leadership styles seem to be effective under different conditions.

There is a relationship between the above research and leadership studies performed by Fred Fiedler, a social psychologist. He discovered that task-oriented and maintenance-oriented leaders performed better according to the needs in a specific situation. He did not find that one type of leadership orientation was effective in *all* situations. In other words, leadership style and orientation are most effective when performed in direct response to a specific situation and group need. For example, a task-oriented leader, one who has a concern that the agenda be completed or the lesson for the day taught, functions best when *on good terms* with the group, when the task to be done is *clearly structured,* and when the leader commands significant *power and authority* in the group. The task-oriented leader is also effective when the leader *directs* the group and/or assumes responsibility for making decisions. In contrast, a maintenance-oriented leader is most effective by *encouraging* decision making by *broad involvement* of the group members. Clearly, situational and contextual differences in groups need to be allowed for in determining what kind of leadership orientation and style would be most helpful. An effective leader will be *flexible* enough *to adjust* herself/himself *to the group* and will seek a *balance* between *getting a job done* by involving others in doing it and *maintenance* needs, such as how people are feeling about doing the task. Group dynamics are far too complex for any one theory or style of group leadership to be effective under all conditions.

Identifying One's Leadership Style

In order to be an effective group leader, it is important to assess one's own leadership style. It is appropriate to ask: Am I more task or maintenance oriented? Do I have reasonable balance between needing to get the task done and the maintenance of the life of the group in my own leadership style? Do I feel more comfortable with one orientation compared to the other? If so, what influence does my orientation have on the group(s) I lead?

Additional questions that need to be asked are: Am I predominantly a democratic, autocratic, or laissez-faire type of leader? What does this type of leadership style do to the group(s) I lead? Am I comfortable with my style or do I want to make any changes in my style? What type of feedback and/or evaluation do I request about my style from groups I lead? How do I feel about being evaluated as a leader? Do I practice what I ask of others? Does a group's reluctance to evaluate itself or me suggest anything special to me about its dynamics?

A person who has developed a democratic style of leadership is most likely one who usually maintains an adequate balance between task and maintenance orientation. If there is an imbalance toward too much maintenance, the designated leader may be leaning toward a laissez-faire style.

In a recent book, *Joining Together Group Theory and Group Skills,* the following exercise was included to enable persons to evaluate their degree of sociability and dominance in interacting with other group members. The instructions follow:

Here are the instructions: There are twenty verbs listed below that describe some of the ways in which people feel and act from time to time. Think of your behavior in groups. How do you feel and act? *Check five verbs below* that best describe your behavior in groups as you see it.

In a group, I:

____Acquiesce	____Concur	____Lead
____Advise	____Criticize	____Oblige
____Agree	____Direct	____Relinquish
____Analyze	____Disapprove	____Resist
____Assist	____Evade	____Retreat
____Concede	____Initiate	____Withdraw
____Coordinate	____Judge	

Two underlying factors or traits are involved in the list of verbs: *dominance* (authority or control) and *sociability* (intimacy or friendliness). Most people tend to like to control things (high dominance) or to let others control things (low dominance). Similarly, most people tend to be warm and personal (high sociability) or to be somewhat cold and impersonal (low sociability). In the [box] below, *circle the five verbs you used* to describe yourself in group activity. The *set* [box] in which *three or more verbs are circled out of the five represents your interpersonal pattern tendency in groups.*[1]

	HIGH DOMINANCE	LOW DOMINANCE
HIGH SOCIABILITY	advise coordinate direct initiate lead	acquiesce agree assist oblige concur
LOW SOCIABILITY	analyze criticize disapprove judge resist	concede evade relinquish retreat withdraw

After determining your dominance-sociability pattern in groups, ask yourself if it is the kind of pattern you want. If not, why not? Are you willing to risk changing?

Analyzing Interpersonal Interactions

One skill a leader needs is an awareness of how persons are interacting within the group process. Robert Bales of Harvard University developed a verbal observation system for persons to observe the extent to which task and maintenance functions actually occur within the group's process. He named it the Interaction Process Analysis System. Readers will note a similarity in Bales' list and the group member task/maintenance functions in chapter 1. The emphasis here, however, is on the role of the designated leader: teacher, chairperson, etc.

As one can see in Figure 1, the first three categories are positive

[1] David W. Johnson and Frank P. Johnson, *Joining Together: Group Theory and Group Skills* (Englewood Cliffs, N.J.: Prentice-Hall, Inc., 1975), pp. 46-47. Italics added. Reprinted by permission of Prentice-Hall, Inc.

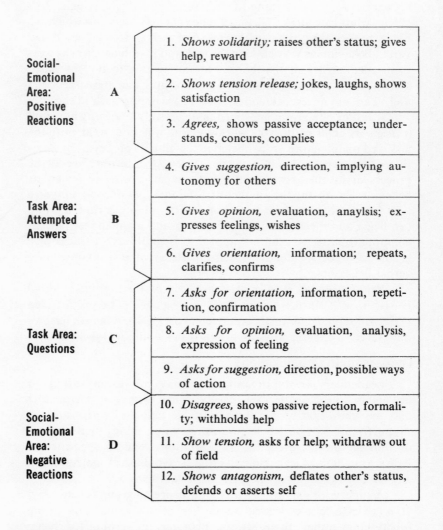

Figure 1—Interaction Process Analysis: Categories and Major Problems (Bales)[2]

[2] Robert F. Bales, "A Set of Categories for the Analysis of Small Group Interaction," *American Sociological Review,* vol. 15 (1950), pp. 257-263, as cited in *The Sociology of Small Groups* by Theodore M. Mills (Englewood Cliffs: Prentice-Hall, Inc., 1967), p. 31. Reprinted by permission of University of Chicago Press.

emotions, while the final three categories represent negative feelings. Categories 4, 5, and 6 stand for task functions which are given to a group, while categories 7, 8, and 9 represent task functions which ask for assistance from others. This blend of task and social-emotional verbal behaviors is very close to the task and maintenance behaviors mentioned earlier in this book. One interesting feature of Bales' system is that the categories are polar opposites; namely, categories 1 and 12 are opposites, categories 2 and 11 are opposites, and so forth.

A leader or a group interested in objectively analyzing how well it meets its goals or does its work will find it helpful to identify the task and maintenance verbal behaviors within its process. The Bales Interaction Process Analysis can be utilized either by observers of the process or by the group itself using a tape recorder to review its behavior. By tallying the number of different types of comments (see tally form in Figure 2) made within a thirty-minute period, a group can begin an objective analysis of its task and maintenance (social-emotional) patterns. Another approach is to observe a leader or a group in order to identify specific patterns of task/maintenance verbal behaviors.

Persons doing even a brief analysis of their group's verbal behaviors will learn whether there is a balance between task and social-emotional comments occurring in the group. A lack of balance may serve to explain why the group is not doing its job well.

Leadership in Organizations

Leadership within organizations may call for a variety of leadership styles. Leadership may be either formal or informal. It may be authoritative or democratic. It may be supervisory or supportive. Indeed, it may be rewarding or punishing by either direct or indirect means. Religious organizations tend to specialize in indirect methods of leadership in order to avoid direct confrontation and/or open conflict in interpersonal relationships.

A supervisor's style has a *direct* influence on group functioning. It is crucial that a leader assess her or his impact on group functioning rather than always blaming the group for being ineffective in some manner. Group process is a two-way dynamic!

The following chart may serve to explain some statements made about leadership earlier in this chapter. The chart is a graphic way of saying that if a leader decides to share decision-making responsibility with the group, the tendency is for the group to increase its participation in making decisions and taking responsibility for them.

To use the chart, begin reading with item 1 on the left and move

Observer Instructions: Simply record a tally mark in a box below whenever you hear such a comment made or see such behavior in the group you are observing.

1. *Shows solidarity,* raises other's status, gives help, reward.					
2. *Shows tension release,* jokes, laughs, shows satisfaction.					
3. *Agrees,* shows passive acceptance, understands, concurs, complies.					
4. *Gives suggestion,* direction, implying autonomy for others.					
5. *Gives opinion,* evaluation, analysis; expresses feeling, wish.					
6. *Gives orientation,* information, repeats, clarifies, confirms.					
7. *Asks for orientation,* information, repetition, confirmation.					
8. *Asks for opinion,* evaluation, analysis, expression of feeling.					
9. *Asks for suggestion,* direction, possible ways of action.					
10. *Disagrees,* shows passive rejection, formality, withholds help.					
11. *Shows tension,* asks for help, withdraws out of field.					
12. *Shows antagonism,* deflates other's status, defends or asserts self.					

          0%   10%   20%   30%   40%   50%

Figure 2—Observer Tally Form [3]

[3] This form developed by Nathan W. Turner, adapted from Bales, *op. cit.*

toward item 7 on the right side of the page. You will see that as the role of the leader becomes one of sharing (and changing leadership style), the role of the group increases in responsibility and in participation. The diagonal line also graphically portrays this shift in responsibility.

Leadership Behavior in Making Decisions[4]

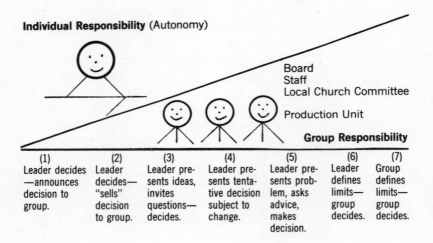

(1)	(2)	(3)	(4)	(5)	(6)	(7)
Leader decides —announces decision to group.	Leader decides— "sells" decision to group.	Leader presents ideas, invites questions— decides.	Leader presents tentative decision subject to change.	Leader presents problem, asks advice, makes decision.	Leader defines limits— group decides.	Group defines limits— group decides.

Summary

In this chapter leadership was defined as a *function* rather than a special kind of personal style. Leadership was also defined as a *learned set of skills*. Leadership functions were noted as the responsibility of the total group.

The theory of functional leadership was briefly described. Research on task/maintenance-oriented types of leaders was cited.

A series of questions about one's own leadership style was included for the leader to reflect on. Next, a special exercise on assessing one's degree of dominance and sociability was included.

The Interaction Process Analysis system and chart developed by Bales was cited as a way for groups and leaders to assess objectively their balance between task and maintenance behavioral patterns.

Finally, a brief section was included on leadership in organizations.

[4] Reprinted with permission of the National Training Laboratories, National Education Association, from the Notebook of the Third Protestant Laboratory on Group Development and Leadership.

CHAPTER 4

Creative Use of Conflict

Conflict is usually regarded as a negative thing by most persons. Within the Christian church we are educated to value peace very highly. Biblically, we are enjoined to forgive others. Repentance, reconciliation, and atonement are familiar terms to church members. Preachers admonish persons for hating, while affirming those who love. Anger is regarded as a "no-no." Hostility between persons is regarded negatively. Conflict in marriage and the family is bad because we are supposed to love and support one another. Conflict within the church is unthinkable, since it appears to contradict our loving heritage. Even more revealing of our value stance against open conflict is the conspicuous absence of material written about conflict by religious institutions and leadership.

Nevertheless, conflict has been occurring within Christendom for centuries in both direct and indirect forms. It is now time for church groups and organizations to acknowledge what has been, is, and will be happening regarding conflict within their ranks. Indeed, it is dehumanizing to deny that a church has conflict and to see the same church split or die years later. The biblical themes of forgiveness, reconciliation, repentance, atonement, and others emphasize that human beings will be in conflict. Perhaps the greatest sins are denial and rationalization.

Conflict occurs whenever people fail to agree on anything. Dealing with conflict begins by recognizing that we have differences. And how we handle our differences says a lot about how we will cope with conflict. Church groups tend to cope poorly and uncreatively with conflict. The purpose of this chapter will be to share a few ideas on how conflict may be utilized in a creative way.

Basic to our whole discussion is a need to examine our values. Unless we can value the creative utilization of conflict, we cannot creatively use its energy and cope with it. Fear will inhibit a group and reduce its problem-solving potential and its progress toward a goal.

Verbal conflict is a *process* characterized by a state of group tension manifested by (1) verbal disagreements (over beliefs, attitudes, values, interests, and information); (2) competition; (3) personal attacks which injure self-esteem; (4) mutually exclusive goals; or (5) a refusal to cope with the preceding verbal conflict.

Interpersonal conflict has many dimensions and many modes. For example, a conflict may be triggered by an old "hidden agenda" (that is, old feelings held over from a prior meeting), occur within the present tense, and carry implications for the future. Consequently, the conflict has several time dimensions alone. The same conflict may also be expressed *directly* (like "I am upset with you!") while the tone of voice communicates an *indirect* message (like "I need you as a friend despite the momentary burst of anger.").

Types of Conflict

Familiar types of conflict in the interpersonal realm of relationships include the following four:

1. *Intrapersonal conflict.* This type of conflict occurs only within the individual. For example, if I have a conflict between two or more of my values, I have an intrapersonal conflict within myself. One problem is that some persons occasionally allow (consciously or unconsciously) an intrapersonal conflict to trigger an interpersonal conflict with another person as a way to reduce one's own internal pressures or unhappiness.

2. *Interpersonal conflict.* This type of conflict occurs between two or more persons. Typical examples would be a marital or family conflict between two or more persons within the marriage/family.

3. *Intragroup conflict.* This type of conflict occurs only in the one group. For example, if a local church board or committee becomes involved in verbal conflict over its own agenda item, it is experiencing *intra*group conflict.

4. *Intergroup conflict.* This type of conflict occurs between two or more groups. An example would be two local church committees disagreeing over who should receive a cut in the annual budget. Or, which committee had the right to decide a specific policy for the church, since both committees had partial responsibility for that area of concern.

Positive and Negative Uses of Conflict

One researcher has noted that most problem-solving groups move through three stages of growth: (1) **orientation** (What is the problem?); (2) **evaluation** (How do we feel about it?) and (3) **control** (What can we do about it?). Conflict may occur at any stage of development; yet the control stage most often serves to trigger interpersonal conflict(s) within a group.

Another researcher identified the initial stage of development as a time of **orientation and testing.** The second stage, **intragroup conflict,** was characterized by hostility, defensiveness, tension, competition, and collapse of group structure.

This background information is included to emphasize that most groups will (or may) go through a stage of conflict on their way to developing fully into a mature and effective group. Any attempt by the leadership to suppress, deny, avoid, or put down a stage of conflict may be a decision to stop the group from fully developing its potential. A positive use of conflict within the group serves to clarify goals and boundaries for the group. A leadership struggle can have positive results when a group tests out what kind of authority it desires and with which type it best functions. To deny or avoid such potentially positive uses of conflict is a negative utilization of the group's power and potential.

Negative uses of conflict occur when persons are attacked, motives impugned, and emotionality is used to cloud real issues. Positive uses include focusing on issues, acceptance of persons without prejudging motives, and a determination to work on one issue at a time without escalating issues together.

Options for Leaders in Utilizing Conflict

Dealing with conflict can be a scary thing for anyone not trained or experienced in coping with it. Since few of us ever have reason to receive formal training in dealing with conflict, what options are available to us when a conflict does arise?

First, there are a number of resource books in print which offer practical help. The Leas and Kittlaus book, *Church Fights, Managing Conflict in the Local Church,* is a good resource. Other books may be found in the bibliography of this book.

Second, it is important to decide whether one is going to cope with the conflict directly, avoid the conflict if possible, or act ambivalently about it. If one decides to cope with the conflict, then a number of options may be considered:

1. Attempt to *define* and describe the conflict *in cooperative terms* (i.e., as a common problem).
2. Try to *deal with issues* rather than personalities.

3. Deal with *one issue at a time.*
4. *Focus on issues while* they are *small* rather than permitting them to grow over time and become large ones.
5. *Attempt to persuade* one another rather than using threats, intimidation, and power plays.
6. Opt for *full disclosure* of all facts rather than allowing "hidden agendas" (leftover feelings or old arguments not settled) to function.
7. Encourage the *validation of* the *other* parties' *interests or concerns* (feelings are valid no matter what the facts are).
8. *Emphasize* what you still hold *in common.*
9. Attempt to portray a *trusting* and *friendly attitude.*
10. Opt for a *"win-win" feeling* (i.e., there is a piece of the pie for each one) rather than a "win-lose" feeling.
11. Attempt to *generate* as many *new ideas* and as much *new information* as possible in order to broaden the perspective of all persons involved.
12. *Involve all* principal *parties* involved in the conflict at a common meeting.
13. Clarify whether you are *dealing with one conflict* or multiple conflicts.

Third, a familiar option is the use of a force field analysis chart to help a group determine the balance of forces moving for a solution to the problem (driving forces) and the forces resisting a solution to the problem (restraining forces). Force field analysis was developed by the late Kurt Lewin, who is considered the father of social psychology in the United States. His idea was that within any group there will be a combination of forces moving for solution to a problem along with powerful forces resisting a solution. Interestingly, in some groups conflict erupts over the fact that some want to solve a problem while others fight against solving the problem, often for hidden reasons.

In order to do a force field analysis, state the problem or conflict across the top of a piece of paper. Next, divide the paper in half and list all the driving forces on the left and all the restraining forces on the right as shown on the next page.

Statement of Problem or Conflict
Requiring a Solution

Driving Forces (+)	Restraining Forces (-)
1.	1.
2.	2.
3.	3.
4.	4.
5.	5.
6.	6.
7.	7.
8.	8.
9.	9.
10.	10.

Next, go back and *underline* any forces, driving or restraining, which you deem most important right now. For each restraining force you underlined, attempt to formulate possible action steps which might reduce or eliminate its negative force against the driving forces. Sometimes brainstorming ideas for action is a quick and efficient way to generate many ideas for action steps.

Now go to the list of driving forces which you underlined and develop possible action steps which might increase and strengthen the force. Again, brainstorming ideas for action may be the quickest and most effective way to develop a maximum number of options for solution.

Review all the steps taken so far and evaluate them. Has anything been missed in haste? Is an action step only going to generate even more restraint from the other side of the field of forces? Determine all resources and leadership available and needed to implement the solution of the conflict.

The key idea behind force field analysis in dealing with conflict is to define the conflict as a *problem held in common* by all persons concerned and requiring a solution. It is important to note that a force field analysis may have more items on one side of the chart than another. The positive and negative *columns do not have to have the same number of items* unless it just happens that way.

Let us take a typical local church problem and show how the force field analysis could be applied to it. The *problem* requiring a solution would be stated as follows:

The Music Budget Needs to Be Cut by 25 Percent Next Year

Forces Favoring a Cut (+)	Forces Against a Cut (-)
1. Income is down from last year.	1. Largest giver favors music.
2. Fewer persons sing in choir.	2. Another children's choir is desired by parents.
3. Music director is not as well trained as we desire.	3. Pastor's wife highly involved in music program.
4. Certain choir members have wanted a separate budget from regular church budget so they could "run their own program."	4. Other items in budget could be cut without reducing music so drastically.
	5. New members are often attracted to our church because of the quality music program we feature.
	6. A new ecumenical music program next year will require a fully funded music program for us to witness to the community.

Having underlined the forces which seem most important right now, let us consider possible action steps to reduce forces one and four on the left side favoring a cut. First, income might be increased through a more vigorous financial canvass of the membership this year. Second, other large givers might be approached to underwrite the music ministry to a larger degree. Third, a meeting could be arranged with the "certain choir members" who want a separate budget in order to listen to their concerns and to try to persuade them to work within regular budget channels.

A similar process of action steps could be developed for the right side of the chart regarding the forces against a cut. Next, review and evaluate all action steps developed so far. Choose action steps which seem most likely to work out and appoint leadership personnel to implement them.

Fourth, another option is to request the services of an outside consultant/trainer to work with the group, organization, or church in dealing with its conflict. It may be that the group has persons already trained in human relations skills and can utilize their expertise as a facilitator to an internal conflict within the group.

The Values Crunch in Conflict Situations

A clash in values (strong beliefs and convictions) between persons and groups often serves as a trigger to conflict. A major crunch in values comes down hard on religious persons who have been raised to avoid conflicts and live a philosophy of "peace at any price." Whereas the field of behavioral sciences places a positive value on constructive/creative conflict, the field of religion has placed a negative value on conflicts of almost any kind.

By reexamining one's traditional religious value on conflict avoidance or conflict denial, the leader can be placed in an internal value conflict. In brief, unless a leader can consciously place a *positive value* on conflict utilization, he or she will tend to avoid, deny, rationalize, or overcontrol the conflict so as to resolve it prematurely. *If* a conflict is *resolved prematurely* (closed off, or superficial agreements reached), then *the conflict will reappear* (recycle) at a later time. Conflict is cyclical in nature and will reappear predictably until the actual roots are dealt with and resolved. Consequently, leader comfort with and valuing of constructive utilization of conflict in groups is a prerequisite for effective group leadership. Usually the first place to begin to get comfortable with conflict is to probe one's value system regarding conflict.

Conflict utilization is a newer notion in the field of conflict studies. The phrase presupposes a positive value placed on a constructive use of conflict. (Clearly no one would value a destructive conflict.) *Utilization* is a dynamic word which is intended to mean that the energy involved in conflict be allowed to *express* itself in constructive ways (i.e., utilized) rather than having a group hold in its strong conflictual feelings and *depress* itself.

It is the purpose of this chapter to challenge the reader to consider a depth reexamination of her or his value system regarding conflict. The average reader may discover a real values crunch between the values one has been raised with and a positive valuing of constructive conflict.

Summary

In this chapter conflict was introduced within a brief biblical-theological context. Conflict was then defined along with a brief description of its nature and four major types of conflict.

A whole section was devoted to positive and negative uses of conflict. A major section of the chapter was devoted to options for leaders in utilizing conflict. Finally, a specific section focused on the values crunch involved for group leaders attempting to cope constructively with conflict in a group. Group leaders may want to consider more formal training in conflict utilization as part of their own development.

CHAPTER 5

Local Church Workshops

Thus far, background material has been presented for the reader to understand the context, stages of development, and leadership styles of groups. At this time, let us focus attention on a series of five local church workshops of two hours duration, each for use within the local congregation or other voluntary organizations using this small book.

The five workshops will cover the following areas:

1. Decision Making
2. Task and Maintenance Functions
3. Leadership Styles and Interventions
4. Values in Conflict
5. Resistance and How to Cope with It

Rationale for Workshops

These workshop outlines are included in the book because of the assumption that we learn best through experience. It is important for the reader to reflect upon how she or he best learns. Is it only through reading that we learn a skill or sport? Or is it through repeated experience and practice?

Based on the belief that we learn best through experience, this chapter is designed so that the workshop leader and participants may learn from one another through the brief experiences outlined herein or through some form of flexible adaptation of these workshop ideas.

Each of the workshops may be held separately on its own or it may be conducted as a series of two or more workshops. This book is to be used as a resource for background and guidance by the church or other organization which is conducting the workshops. Each session is completely outlined within this chapter as an aid to the leader. After carefully planning for each session, the leader will conduct the session for the group members.

Instructions to Workshop Leaders

Leader Preparation

Each workshop leader is asked to read this entire book as background for the workshop. The leader may then decide what chapter content he or she may desire to duplicate for workshop members to read as background. Key ideas of background material for the workshop participants to read and think about can be written on newsprint or chalkboard. Certainly, every workshop participant would be ideally prepared if he or she read this entire book as preparation also. Page references to key portions of the book for additional background reading are given in the workshop instructions. Finally, workshop leaders may desire to read some of the additional books listed in the bibliography. Leaders may duplicate copies of any forms or charts in this book for use in their workshop sessions.

Workshop Times

The suggested amounts of time for each portion of each workshop are only approximations. In some cases, the time may be just right. In other instances, leaders may need to lengthen the time if workshop participants desire more time for discussion of the topic involved. In brief, *be flexible in adjusting workshop times* as needed.

Size of Groups

The suggested number of twelve persons in a workshop is only intended as a suggestion. Obviously, you may have less or more than twelve in a given workshop and you will wonder, "What do I do now?" Here are some suggestions for making each workshop flexible regardless of the number of persons who attend. *First,* if you have more than twelve persons, you may assign a few more to the role of observer. If you have twenty-four persons, you can run two simultaneous workshops by giving each group the same instructions. Then you can move from one group to another and give them guidance. Or, you can arrange for a second person to work with the second group of twelve. *Second,* if you have less than twelve persons participating, perhaps only six to eight persons, you may decide to postpone the workshop until you can secure twelve or more persons. You may decide to combine your workshop with that of another nearby church and share leadership with a friend from another church. You may decide to proceed with the workshop, using whatever number you have. For example, a group of seven persons could be arranged as follows for workshop 1: a group of four could be designated the committee to decide on teaching time. The other three persons could be given combined observer assignments, with one person observing for questions 1 and 2, a second person observing for questions 3 and 4, and a third person observing for question 5.

Each subsequent workshop in this chapter may be conducted with fewer than twelve persons by simply allocating fewer persons to each assignment and by combining assignments to each person or by eliminating certain questions or assignments if they do not appear practical for your church.

Physical Arrangements

Physically arranging the room is an important part of the workshop leader's responsibilities. Personally checking the room for adequate heating/cooling, lighting, seating (circles are an ideal arrangement) for everyone expected, paper/pencil supplies, newsprint, markers, crayons, tape, tacks, scissors, chalk and chalkboards, and name tags for everyone. Coffee, tea, and snacks may be desired also.

Getting Acquainted

It is assumed that most persons attending a local church workshop will know one another already. If so, please feel free to minimize time needed to help persons get acquainted. However, if persons do not know one another, workshop leaders may desire to include an additional thirty minutes for getting-acquainted time. Having persons talk in *twos* about their favorite vacation places, the most exciting times they have ever had, what they like most about their church, and background on their families or jobs are usually winners for helping people start getting acquainted. Another option is to have persons talk in twos for ten minutes and then take one minute to introduce that person to the total group and vice versa. Leader discretion will be needed in deciding whether or not getting-acquainted time is needed. If so, be sure to include the necessary time in the estimated workshop schedule for this important process.

Leader Options

Additional leader options for any of the workshops may include using a *role play* instead of any of the discussion suggested. Or a leader may desire to have part of an actual church board/committee meeting *tape-recorded* (with permission, of course) and play an actual segment for the workshop session to analyze in light of the questions posed in each workshop topic area. Another option would be for the leader personally to write up a brief *case study* of a board/committee discussion for workshop participants to study and analyze. Or, the leader might ask a member of a board/committee to write up such a segment of a meeting and share it with the workshop (any one of the five workshops).

Workshop Observers

It is important for the workshop leader to type out and duplicate copies of all instructions and questions for the *observers* in each workshop. Instructions and questions are contained within each workshop description in this chapter. Specifically, the main assignment to communicate to each observer is that they are to *watch for and record in writing* samples of any statements they hear related to the specific question assigned to them.

Workshop Final Discussion

During the final discussion time in each of the five workshops, the leader will want to guide the group in asking: (1) How has this experience been helpful to me personally? (2) How has this experience been helpful to my board, committee, or group? and (3) How will this experience be helpful to my church or organization?

WORKSHOP 1

Decision Making

An **effective** decision involves the following characteristics:

1. A clear definition of *the issue* about which the group needs to make a decision;

2. A willingness of the group to state and work through major questions and reservations about the decision before it is made, carefully analyzing the blocks to the decision during the process of making it;

3. A consideration of a variety of *alternatives* and selection of the best alternative with plans for implementation;

4. A utilization of the resources (such as knowledge and skills) of the group members;

5. An acceptance of the decision by the group with a willingness to support and carry out the decision;

6. An assignment of an expected *time* for the implementation of the decision along with the assignment of who will be responsible;

7. An agreement upon an *evaluation* process.

Common causes of blocks to effective decision making include:

1. Past *history* of the group which involves unresolved issues and feelings;

2. A *struggle* for leadership and power among group members and between group members and the leader;

3. *Fear* of the implications and consequences of the decision;

4. *Inappropriate methods* of decision making for the particular situation (being dictatorial when people were expecting a democratic method);

5. *Assumptions* and *expectations* which are not checked out;

6. *Inattention* to group *resistance,* conflict, doubt, and questions.

Leader Assignment

For this workshop the leader will want to read chapters 1, 2, 3, and 4 of the book carefully. Duplicate copies of Form 1, entitled "Checklist on Decision Making," for all participants. Form 2, entitled "Checklist of Participants' Responsibilities in Group Discussion," may be duplicated for members of workshop 1. Form 2 may also be used as a general background resource for members of all five workshops if so desired.

Outline for Workshop on Decision Making (two hours)

Purpose:

To discover through practice what aids or hinders effective decision making.

Step 1 (thirty minutes):

Ask a maximum of seven people to work as a committee. The decision to be made is whether or not to lengthen the church school teaching time by forty-five minutes per week. If another type of decision is more relevant to your group, substitute it.

Ask the remaining persons to *observe the discussion* in these five specific ways: (1) *what* seems to *facilitate* the group making the decision? (2) *what* seems to *block* the group from making the decision? (3) *what* types of *questions* are asked? (4) what *feelings* are expressed (like anger, frustration, doubt, confidence, etc.)? and (5) *who* speaks to *whom*? Each of the five observers should take careful notes of *actual behaviors,* including specific quotes or instances of behavior actually observed.

It will be helpful if the leader writes these five questions on chalkboard or newsprint or has a copy for each observer.

Step 2 (twenty-five minutes):

Have each of the observers share her or his observations with the group of seven for a maximum of five minutes per observer.

Step 3 (fifteen minutes):

Ask the group to resume the original discussion in light of the observer feedback just heard. The task is to try to reach a decision by incorporating the feedback just received.

Step 4 (twenty minutes):

Each of the observers shares a second round of observations for only four minutes per observer with the group.

Step 5 (twenty-five minutes):

The total group has a general discussion regarding what has been observed and learned about effective decision making in a group. (See the characteristics of effective decision making listed at the opening of this workshop.)

Give participants copies of Form 1, "Checklist on Decision Making." Suggest that individuals rate themselves. Then in triads (groups of three people) individuals can check their perception of themselves with how the other two people see them.

If more time is desired, a group could agree to meet a second time on another date, repeat the above process, and attempt to go further by selecting another type of problem which it faces and using the observer feedback process as suggested.

Step 6 (five minutes):

The leader may wish to share with the group the information on decision making found at the beginning of this workshop.

Form 1

Checklist on Decision Making

The decisions you make for your own personal needs are important to you. Treat them with care by using the same methods social scientists recommend for group decision making.

PERSONAL CHECKLIST

In my decision processes I follow the procedure of:	Most of the time	Some of the time	Need to improve
1. Analyzing the problem in terms of all possible factors . . .			
2. Determining what my own motives are in recommending (or fighting) a change . . .			
3. Identifying (where possible) the feelings of others involved . . .			
4. Gathering as much objective information as I can before evaluating . . .			
5. Looking at my own skills of perception and analysis . . .			
6. Creating an atmosphere where others can differ from me . . .			
7. Checking during the implementation stage with a readiness to revise the original decision . . .			

Form 2

Checklist of Participants' and Leader's Responsibilities in Group Discussion

Preparation

  A. Group Participants:

    1. Prepare to discuss.

    2. Arrive on time.

  B. Leader:

    1. Arranges for physical setting.

      —chairs and tables for all (no second row seats)
      —temperature and lighting
      —chalkboard, chalk, and eraser, or butcher paper and crayon
      —name cards and crayons, if necessary

    2. Prepares tentative outline.

    3. Prepares some questions in advance of meeting.

      —to get discussion started
      —to keep discussion going purposefully
      —to help keep discussion related to experience of participants
      —to bring out all sides of topic

Discussion

  A. Leader:

    1. Begins on time.

    2. Introduces the topic.

      —suggests purpose of discussion
      —presents tentative outline
      —allows time for participants to adjust outline if necessary

    3. Records participants' thoughts concisely on chalkboard or chart pad.

    4. Erases contributions, with permission.

    5. Draws all participants into discussion as soon as possible.

6. Helps people communicate when necessary.

7. Guides group to minimize useless speculation.

8. Gives "thought-flow" summaries when needed (repetition, domination, clarification).

9. Keeps discussion on track (if desirable).

10. Remains neutral.

11. Does not become the center of attention by making speeches, standing unnecessarily, encouraging teacher-pupil atmosphere, commenting on each contribution, or sitting apart from the group.

B. Group Participants:

1. Help adjust leader's outline.

2. Make contributions in the language of the group.

3. Bring out all sides of the question.

4. Accept and support each other as unique individuals.

5. Try to prevent domination of the discussion.

6. Help each other understand what is said.

7. Add to each other's contributions spontaneously.

8. Build upon others' contributions (avoid leaving contributions dangling).

9. Listen actively.

10. Help keep discussion on the track.

11. Draw other participants into the discussion.

Closing

A. Leader:

1. Stops discussion on time or before interest wanes.

2. Presents final summary of consensus and of differing opinions.

B. Group Participants:

1. Adjust leader's summary (if necessary).

2. Plan next meeting: leader, topic, materials to study, date.

WORKSHOP 2

Task/Maintenance Functions

Groups usually assemble for a purpose. An immediate *task* of a group is to define its purpose and clarify for all present why everyone is there. The task of a group is normally the stated business (task) or purpose for which persons have agreed to meet and work together.

Task functions which enable a group to function effectively were described on page 13 of chapter 1. Summarized they are:

1. *Initiate*—suggesting of new ideas, methods, or solutions in order to enable the group to fulfill its task.

2. *Clarify*—asking questions or making statements which assist the group to move towards its goal(s). It can mean checking out assumptions and expectations which have not been shared up to a given point in the discussion.

3. *Analyze*—dividing broader issues and problems into smaller, more workable steps for discussion and solution.

4. *Summarize*—pulling together the loose ends. A summary statement enables a group to realize where it is and how much it has accomplished.

5. *Seek Information and Opinions*—seeking additional information or opinions in order to clarify values and opinions previously stated within the group.

Within a group, members have many feelings and needs; yet seldom are these expressed in a work group or committee meeting. In order for a group to function smoothly and effectively, a healthy emotional climate needs to be maintained and attended to: hence, the term *maintenance* function.

Maintenance functions within a group may include the following functions which do get interwoven with the ongoing task functions on the basis of group need:

These functions were described on pages 13-14 of chapter 1.

1. *Keep the Gate*—keeping communication open and flowing, the facilitation of the flow of conversation, seeing that all persons have an opportunity to speak or to support a minority viewpoint.

2. *Encourage*—expressing warmth and responsiveness to other group members. It also means *building* upon other's ideas.

3. *Listen*—listening actively to the group conversation without participating in or attending to other distractions or fringe talk.

4. *Harmonize*—reconciling differences, relieving tension, and diplomatically exploring reasons for differences.

5. *Set Standards*—suggesting standards for group use in selecting content or methods. It may also include suggesting that the group evaluate its decisions or processes.

It is important to note that typical nonfunctional group roles may include blocking, aggressiveness, status seeking, dominating, hidden agendas, and special-interest persons pushing only one area of "pet" interest.

Leader Assignment

Read chapters 1 and 3. Duplicate for this workshop Form 3 entitled "How I Perceived the Person."

Outline for Workshop on Task and Maintenance Functions
(two hours)
Purpose:

To discover through practice how the use of the task and maintenance functions helps a group and to discover how they are interrelated.

Step 1 (thirty minutes):

Divide the total group into a discussion group with at least three persons serving as observers. If the group is too large for a good discussion, say more than seven to nine people, have more persons take the role of observers. Have the persons who are to be the discussion group select a task or a maintenance role which they will practice by pulling out of a box slips of paper on which a role has been written. One of the slips of paper will indicate that the person is to play a nonfunctional negative or blocking role.

The observers will each observe only one type of role—task, maintenance, or the blocking role. The observers are asked to keep actual quotes of what was said and what happened during the discussion. Form 3 may be used here.

Step 2 (fifteen minutes):

Each observer shares his or her observations for a maximum of five minutes each with the group.

Step 3 (fifteen minutes):

The discussion group responds to the three observers' feedback for fifteen minutes by trying to use the roles more effectively or asking questions about the task or maintenance role.

Step 4 (thirty minutes):

A general discussion of the importance of and problems with task and maintenance functions, as the group sees them, in the ongoing work of their group or organization.

Step 5 (fifteen minutes):

Each of the observers again provides a maximum of five minutes feedback from their observations of the discussion in Step 4.

Step 6 (fifteen minutes):

The total group has a general discussion about task and maintenance functions summarizing what they have learned about them during this workshop. Members may be encouraged to identify roles they will wish to put into practice in boards or committee meetings as well as study groups they are in. The leader of the workshop gives additional input from chapter 1 of this book.

WORKSHOP 3

Leadership Styles and Interventions

For the purpose of this workshop, let us define *leadership as a series of functions,* including task/maintenance functions, which members are to provide, required for a group to function effectively and reach its goals. Clearly, then, leadership is a function which can be provided by one person, by several persons within a group, or by each person in the group. Ideally, in church and voluntary organizational groups, leadership is a series of functions provided by many persons involved in the group, including the designated leader. The more widely leadership functions are shared, the broader the base of group responsibility developed among the members. As was said in chapter 3, the functional theory of leadership presumes that leadership is an acquired set of skills which most anyone can learn, given a few minimal basic skills within that person (like an ability to communicate clearly and an ability to assert oneself).

Leadership interventions are any questions, statements, emotions, selected silences, or changes in leadership style which influence

Form 3

How I Perceived the Person

Task-Maintenance Functions	Comments:	Group-Maintenance Functions	Comments:
1. **Initiation:** Proposing tasks or goals, defining a group problem, suggesting a procedure or ideas for solving a problem.		1. **Encouraging:** Being friendly, warm, and responsive to others; accepting others and their contributions; regarding others by giving them an opportunity for recognition.	
2. **Information or opinion seeking:** Requesting facts, seeking relevant information about a group concern, asking for suggestions and ideas.		2. **Expressing group feelings:** Sensing feeling, mood, relationships within the group; sharing own feeling or effect with other member.	
3. **Information or opinion giving:** Offering facts, providing relevant information about group concern, stating a belief, giving suggestions or ideas.		3. **Harmonizing:** attempting to reconcile disagreements, reducing tensions through "pouring oil on troubled waters," getting people to explore their differences.	
4. **Clarifying or elaborating:** Interpreting or reflecting ideas and suggestions, clearing up confusions, indicating alternatives and issues before the group, giving examples.		4. **Compromising:** When own idea or status is involved in a conflict, offering to compromise own position; admitting error, disciplining self to maintain group cohesion.	
5. **Summarizing:** Pulling together related ideas, restating suggestions after group has discussed them, offering a decision or conclusion for the group to accept or reject.		5. **Gate-keeping:** Attempting to keep communication channels open, facilitating the participation of others, suggesting procedures for sharing opportunity to discuss group problems.	
6. **Consensus tester:** Sending up trial balloons to see if group is nearing a conclusion, checking with group to see how agreement has been reached.		6. **Setting standards:** Expressing standards for group to achieve, applying standards in evaluating group function and production.	

a group to move toward its goal(s). Hence, any person within the group may make a leadership intervention into the group process.

Leader Assignment

Read chapter 3 carefully. Duplicate copies of the diagram "Leadership Behavior in Making Decisions" in chapter 3 and "Some Suggestions to Members of Discussion Groups," Form 4 in this chapter. These copies of Form 4 may be distributed in the workshop.

Outline for Workshop on Leadership Styles and Interventions
(two hours)
Purpose:

To discover through practice what different leadership styles and interventions can do to a group.

Step 1 (thirty-five minutes):

In advance of the workshop, the leader asks three persons to volunteer or selects three persons to help with the workshop. Each of these persons is to demonstrate a different style of leadership: autocratic, democratic, laissez-faire, with the group. (If necessary, the leader of the workshop could demonstrate all three styles.)

Give each person a description of the style you wish her or him to demonstrate. Also make some suggestions about the kind of situation in which the demonstration is to take place. For example, the chairperson or a board or committee (select a specific one) or a church school teacher leading a class session. The autocratic teacher has prepared a lesson and is determined to teach it regardless of what the members of the class may desire. Or, the autocratic board chairperson may or may not ask persons' opinions, but makes all the final decisions. The democratic leader encourages all to speak on the issues, plans for action from the suggestions, attempts to get consensus rather than a vote on an issue. As a church school teacher, the democratic leader encourages all viewpoints to be expressed. The laissez-faire leader may come into the group asking, "What do you want to do today?" and sitting and waiting for the group to take responsibility.

Before each demonstration, the leader describes the situation and members are asked to role-play the situation with the appointed person acting a leader.

Step 2 (fifteen minutes):

After the demonstrations, members of the group share how they feel about the different styles demonstrated. Use the following guidelines: (1) identify the leadership styles demonstrated; (2) express feelings about the leadership styles (what was going on inside of the persons during each demonstration); (3) identify what happens to a group when the different styles of leadership are used. For instance, what are the coping patterns of the members (fight, flight, denial, etc.)?

Step 3 (ten minutes):

Divide the group into small groups of three persons each. Ask one group to discuss what they like or don't like about the autocratic leadership style and make suggestions as to when this style might be appropriate. Similarly, have a second group discuss the pros and cons of a laissez-faire leadership style. When is this style appropriate? Ask a third group to deal similarly with the democratic style. If you have more than nine people, two triads could work on the same leadership style.

Step 4 (ten minutes):

Each group will share with the total group a summary of its discussion.

Step 5 (twenty minutes):

The total group will have a discussion regarding what the different styles and interventions can do to a group. The discussion may be partially focused on where the different leadership styles may be helpful within the life of a group or organization. The diagram on leadership behavior in chapter 3 may help to facilitate this discussion. Copies of this can be distributed to each member.

Step 6 (thirty minutes):

Take the group through the exercise on pages 23-24 of chapter 3. The list of words can be put on newsprint or chalkboard, with persons writing their own list, or each person can be given a duplicated copy of the list.

Form 4

Some Suggestions to Members of Discussion Groups

1. Come prepared to take responsibility for making a good discussion group, to share ideas, questions, and information as well as to listen. All parasites and no participants makes a dull group. If you have come along "just for the ride" or just "to see what is going on," you will profit most as a *participant* observer who experiences what is going on.

2. Be seated so you can see the faces of every other member of the group. Avoid back rows and "sleeper play" locations.

3. Wear your name tag until you can call everyone by his or her name and *practice using the names of others in the discussion.*

4. Talk briefly and to the point. *Stay on the topic. Avoid speeches.* Don't take over the floor and keep it. No filibusters or long personal reminiscences, please.

5. After you have spoken, pause until others have had a chance to talk. Some are not as "fast on the draw" as others.

6. Do not worry about silence. People may be thinking. This is usually a good thing.

7. *Try to listen to what the other person is really trying to say.* See if you can rephrase accurately in your own words what was said. Test your perceptions occasionally by repeating what you thought the person said and ask if that is correct. If you do not understand a word or an idea or a suggestion, say so. Ask the person to try explaining it again or to give an illustration.

8. If another person is having trouble making a point, perhaps you can help him or her to clarify it. If a person is trying to get a word in edgewise and is crowded out, help that person to get the floor. If someone is timid or hesitant to speak, give encouragement. *But don't rush in to finish sentences for others.*

9. Differences can be creative. Controversy may be a stimulus to a deeper study of the problem. To insist on conformity or to close out discussion too quickly may block the Holy Spirit.

10. Speak the truth (as you see it) in love. *Reject ideas* or disagree, but *do not reject persons.*

WORKSHOP 4

Conflict in Values

A value is a belief, attitude, conviction, activity, or feeling that satisfies the following seven criteria: "(1) having been freely chosen, (2) having been chosen from among alternatives, (3) having been chosen after due reflection, (4) having been prized and cherished, (5) having been publicly affirmed, (6) having been incorporated into actual behavior, and (7) having been repeated in one's life."[1] One's personal values regarding groups, persons, decision making, task and maintenance functions, leadership styles, conflict, and how to cope with group resistance are components of how one will function within a small group.

When the value(s) of one person conflict with those of others in the group, there are some common ways members usually react. These include fighting, taking flight, denying, agreeing, or compromising.

Leader Assignment

Read chapters 3 and 4 especially. Duplicate Form 5, entitled "Verbal Conflict Observer Form," for all observers in this workshop. If participants have not been in Workshop 2, you will want to duplicate Forms 2 and 3. Also, duplicate copies of Form 3, entitled "How I Perceived the Person," for each participant's background information.

Outline for Workshop of Conflict in Values (two hours)
Purpose:

To discover through practice ways a group usually reacts to a values conflict and to consider alternative ways to react if needed.

Step 1 (thirty minutes):

Select several persons (two or three, depending on the size of the group) to serve as observers. Ask the remaining members to hold a discussion about one of the following issues: (1) whether to include $500 in the budget for the minister's continuing education, (2) whether to cut the Christian education budget by $1,000, or (3) whether all new members must give a profession of faith to the deacons before they can be admitted as members. Ask the three

[1] L. E. Raths, M. Harmin, and S. B. Simon, *Values and Teaching: Working with Values in the Classroom* (Columbus: Charles E. Merrill Publishing Company, 1966), p. 46.

observers to watch for verbal patterns of (1) fight (to fight/argue verbally), (2) flight (to change subject verbally or to leave room physically or psychologically), (3) denial (to deny conflict is occurring), and (4) agreement (to agree to most anything momentarily so as to avoid a conflict or argument). Observers should take notes and record actual quotes where possible. The observers may use Form 5, "Verbal Conflict Observer Form."

Step 2 (fifteen minutes):

The observers give feedback to the discussion group (five minutes per observer) on what they observed in terms of their assigned observation role as given above.

Step 3 (thirty minutes):

Group resumes its original discussion while integrating any learnings from the feedback just received in Step 2. A new subject can be picked if it seems more profitable or interesting.

Step 4 (fifteen minutes):

Again, the observers give feedback to the group. Special attention will be given to any changes in their ability to cope with differences when their conflict is in relation to their values (five minutes per observer).

Step 5 (twenty-five minutes):

The total group enters into a discussion to: (1) identify learnings about how values conflict within a group, (2) identify what they discovered about their personal coping patterns when there is conflict with their values, and (3) identify what each coping pattern accomplished in the group.

Ask each person to identify what each would do differently if faced with a similar situation.

Step 6 (five minutes):

The leader shares with the group some of the highlights of chapter 4.

Form 5

Verbal Conflict Observer Form

Instructions to Observer: As you use this form, please make a tally mark in the appropriate box next to one of the four categories you believe you have just observed in the group of persons you are assigned to watch. Please write in an example of any quote you can recall which illustrates what you observed in any category below.

	Record tally here:	Write sample of comment here:
Fight—to fight verbally, argue, disagree, or discount.		
Flight—to change subject verbally, to leave room physically, or to withdraw psychologically.		
Denial—to deny that any verbal conflict is occurring.		
Agreement/Compromise—to agree to almost anything, momentarily, so as to avoid a conflict or argument at the moment.		

WORKSHOP 5

Resistance and How to Cope with It

Resistance within a group means to resist the leadership, the issues under discussion, the decision about to be made, or another person(s) within the group who wants to change something. Symptoms of resistance may include apathy, boredom, indifference, anger, confusion, or stalling/blocking behaviors to delay action. Resistance can be scary to deal with, since few of us are experienced in dealing with it directly. Resistance can delay a group when it is not dealt with directly and the resistance is permitted to run its course. If never dealt with, resistance can be destructive to a group or organization.

First, it is important to recognize that resistance is a symptom and not a cause. It is really a message to the group and its leadership that something else is going on, but not being dealt with. Common causes of resistance are fear of change, lack of ownership in a decision, fear of losing one's power or position of influence in the group. If the message is listened to, the group life will be maintained by openly *switching from a task to a maintenance function* level immediately. Then, when the real problem has been handled, the group can move on.

Second, beginning to talk about the group resistance is the best way to begin coping with it. For example, persons who are invariably late to a group meeting or leave early from a group are resisters. Their lack of presence does influence, often negatively, the group process and progress in reaching the group goal.

Third, resistance is often denied. Consequently, it is important to focus on the behavior evidenced rather than only on persons per se. For example, there have to be reasons why the whole group or a portion acts bored!

Fourth, resistance can be openly confronted if it is approached in terms of how we *appear* to be using our energy and how we feel about it. Ask: "Are there alternatives to what has been happening for us to consider?" "Is there a new way to behave that would be more productive and effective for us as a group?"

Leader Assignment

Read chapters 3 and 4 and 2 in that order. Duplicate copies of Form 6, entitled "Observer Form on Group Resistance," for use by the observers.

Outline for Workshop on Resistance and How to Cope with It
(two hours)
Purpose:

To discover through practice the causes of resistance and what resistance can mean to a group and to consider new ways with which to cope with it.

Step 1 (thirty minutes):

The group will participate in a role play. The situation for the role play is a meeting of the membership committee of a church. The chairperson has called the meeting to consider some plan to try to enlist into active participation in the life of the church a group of members who have become inactive in attendance. Some of these people still give money to the church, but others are not contributing. The task of the group in the role play is to "develop a plan that will reenlist these people into active membership."

The leader will prepare small pieces of paper so that each member of the group will receive one. One piece of paper will say, "You are the chairperson"; three will say, "You are an observer"; half of the remaining will say, "You are to be positive and enthusiastic about the church and the people who are not attending"; and the other half of the remaining will say, "You are to be very negative about both the church and the people who are not attending."

The observers are to use Form 6 as a guide in their observation. They will report in Step 2.

When the role play is ready to begin, the leader sets the scene by reading the situation given above. When the role play is finished, have the various members tell how they are feeling right now.

Step 2 (fifteen minutes):

The three observers will then give feedback to the group on their observations (five minutes per observer).

Step 3 (thirty minutes):

The group will continue its role play. This time the enthusiasts will try to cope openly with the resistance of the apathetic resisting persons.

Step 4 (twenty-five minutes):

The members each tell how they are feeling right now. The observers again give feedback to the group indicating any differences in coping with resistance that they noted.

Step 5 (fifteen minutes):

In the total group, individuals will identify learnings about group resistance and how to cope with it. It is important to discuss feelings of all concerned and what might have been done differently in order to cope with resistance more effectively.

Step 6 (five minutes):

The leader shares with the group the information about resistance in groups which is found at the beginning of this workshop.

Form 6

Observer Form on Group Resistance

Instructions to Observer: As you use this form, please make a tally mark in the appropriate box next to one of the three categories you believe you have just observed (heard/seen) in the group of persons you are assigned to watch. Please write in an example of any quote you can recall which illustrates what you observed in any category below.

	Record tally here:	Write sample comments here:
Verbal Resistance—lack of group discussion, including prolonged silences which feel uncomfortable; changing the subject; apathy; disinterest; challenging types of questions which cause confusion or group uneasiness.		
Nonverbal resistance—arms crossed, bored expressions, depressed expressions, leaving early or arriving late, permitting numerous phone interruptions, shuffling of feet, tapping of fingers on table.		
Coping with resistance—persons who **ask** questions about verbal or nonverbal forms of resistance, **suggest** group discuss when it feels resistance is occurring, make **suggestions** regarding an improvement in group norms, **confront** specific persons regarding their apparent resistance, give **feedback** to resisters if they request it.		

Bibliography

Cartwright, Darwin, and Zander, Alvin, eds., *Group Dynamics: Research and Theory,* 3rd ed. (New York: Harper & Row, Publishers, 1968).

Day, LeRoy, *Dynamic Christian Fellowship,* rev. ed. (Valley Forge: Judson Press, 1968).

Deutsch, M., "Conflicts: Productive and Destructive," *Journal of Social Issues,* vol. 25 (1969), pp. 7-43.

Dow, Robert A., *Learning Through Encounter* (Valley Forge: Judson Press, 1971).

Johnson, David W., and Johnson, F. P., *Joining Together: Group Theory and Group Skills* (Englewood Cliffs, N.J.: Prentice-Hall, Inc., 1975).

Johnson, David W., *Reaching Out: Interpersonal Effectiveness and Self Actualization* (Englewood Cliffs, N.J.: Prentice-Hall, Inc., 1972).

Leas, Speed, and Kittlaus, Paul, *Church Fights: Managing Conflict in the Local Church* (Philadelphia: The Westminister Press, 1973).

Lewin, Kurt, *Resolving Social Conflicts,* ed. Gertrud Weiss Lewin (New York: Harper & Row, Publishers, 1948).

Leypoldt, Martha M., *Learning Is Change* (Valley Forge: Judson Press, 1971).

_____, *40 Ways to Teach in Groups* (Valley Forge: Judson Press, 1967).

Luft, Joseph, *Group Processes: An Introduction to Group Dynamics,* rev. ed. (Palo Alto, Calif.: National Press Books, 1970).

McGregor, D., *The Human Side of Enterprise* (New York: McGraw-Hill Book & Education Services Group, 1960).

Raths, L. E.; Harmin, M.; and Simon, S. B., *Values and Teaching: Working with Values in the Classroom* (Columbus, Ohio: Charles E. Merrill Publishing Company, 1966).

Reid, Clyde, *Groups Alive, Church Alive: The Effective Use of Small Groups in the Local Church* (New York: Harper & Row, Publishers, 1969).

Schutz, William C., *The Interpersonal Underworld* (Palo Alto, Calif.: Science and Behavior Books, Inc., 1966).

Watson, Goodwin, and Johnson, David W., *Social Psychology: Issues and Insights* (Philadelphia: J. B. Lippincott Company, 1972).